TINY OWL™

AND THE ROCKEFELLER CHRISTMAS TREE

Inspired by a true story

Deborah, Gianna, and Lea Rocco
Illustrated by Nataliia Tymoshenko

This is Tiny Owl. She is only seven inches tall and is not much bigger than a Christmas ball. She is of the Northern Saw—whet owl breed and likes to sleep in the evergreen trees. She sleeps by day and travels by night. She has a catlike face and big yellow eyes.

How did she come to capture our hearts?

This is where the story starts.

You see, Tiny Owl fell asleep in this very big tree. What Tiny Owl didn't know is that this Norway spruce was the one chosen for the iconic Rockefeller Christmas Tree! What is so special about this tree? Once a year it is on display for the whole world to see.

Then one cold November day, Tiny Owl became trapped in the tree and taken away.

The tree was cut down and placed on a truck. Before she could fly away, Tiny Owl became trapped and stuck. The truck traveled from Oneonta, NY to New York City, a long, 170-mile journey.

Tiny Owl was scared but brave and didn't know what to think. She went three whole days without any food to eat or water to drink.

When the tree arrived at Rockefeller Center Plaza, Tiny Owl was discovered!

Imagine the worker's surprise when he saw Tiny Owl and her bright yellow eyes. The worker was a big man with gentle hands. He rescued Tiny Owl from the tree and held her close so she would not flee.

To keep her safe, Tiny Owl was placed in a box. It didn't take long for the story to hit all of the big news outlets, including CNN, BBC, and fox.

Tiny Owl's discovery in this famous tree caused a media frenzy. Some called Tiny Owl "he," "she," "Rockefeller," and "Rocky." Some even called her a "stowaway" and the "Christmas Miracle of 2020." Tiny Owl has no home or no name, but this Christmas, Tiny Owl gained a lot of attention and fame.

Since it had been quite an adventure, Tiny Owl was brought to the Ravensbeard Wildlife Center. She was wrapped in a blanket to keep her warm. She was given a checkup and an x-ray to see if she was healthy and strong. After a few days of rest and care, the veterinarian said she was in the clear and there was no need to keep her here.

Tiny Owl was released into the wild at dusk, the time when owls usually wake up. Before Tiny Owl took flight, she was wished a very long and happy life.

Tiny Owl flew beautifully to the nearest pine tree.

After five minutes she decided to leave.

Where to now, Tiny Owl?

Tiny Owl will travel hundreds of miles

south during the cold winter months.

Although she is free and there are many places to see, Tiny Owl returns every year to celebrate the wonder of Christmas in New York City.

Is that her yellow eyes you see, or is it the lights of the Rockefeller Christmas Tree?

This book is dedicated to the everyday heroes
who help others, large and small.